EVERYTHING A MAN SHOULD BE

ALSO FROM REVIVAL TODAY

Dominion Over Sickness and Disease

Boldly I Come

Twenty Secrets for an Unbreakable Marriage

How to Dominate in a Wicked Nation

Seven Wrong Relationships

Everything a Man Should Be

Books are available in EBOOK and PAPERBACK through your favorite online book retailer or by request from your local book store.

EVERYTHING A MAN SHOULD BE

8 THINGS MY FATHER SHOWED ME THAT PRODUCED A BLESSED LIFE

JONATHAN SHUTTLESWORTH

Unless otherwise indicated, all Scripture quotations are taken from the Holy Bible, New Living Translation, copyright © 1996, 2004, 2015 by Tyndale House Foundation. Used by permission of Tyndale House Publishers, a Division of Tyndale House Ministries, Carol Stream, Illinois 60188. All rights reserved.

Book design by eBook Prep
www.ebookprep.com

June 2022
ISBN: 978-1-64457-283-2

Rise UP Publications

644 Shrewsbury Commons Ave
Ste 249
Shrewsbury PA 17361
United States of America
www.riseUPpublications.com
Phone: 866-846-5123

CONTENTS

To my father, Evangelist Tiff Shuttlesworth.

INTRODUCTION

When I received an invitation to speak at a prison for the first time, the second I got up to speak, I could tell in my spirit there was an immediate disconnect between the prisoners and I. I'm sure they were thinking, "This works for you and whatever nice world you grew up in, but it's different here." So, the Holy Spirit gave me something to say right in the beginning. "Just so you know, if you had my parents, you would be standing here giving the message. And if I had your parents, I would most likely be sitting where you're at." Of course, there are people who backslide, and some are hell-bent regardless of who their parents are. You can look at the statistics and see that incarceration is not discriminatory based on race. Rather, the number of incarcerations follows the number of homes without fathers present. The lowest incarceration rates are among South Koreans and Jewish people, who have the highest rate of fathers in the home.

The welfare system was set up to destroy the home. The government will actually pay people in communities to not get married. For example, if a woman marries the man that fathered her child, she loses her welfare-provided income and housing. It's a satanic manipulation of money to break down communities. But, be encouraged because the power of God will undue every wicked plan in Washington DC to destroy homes.

It would have been impossible for me to not turn out serving the Lord and loving God with all my heart. I was raised in a home where my dad didn't just preach in the pulpit—he lived it out. While the media has made you feel like every preacher is a fraud, I saw my mom and dad in and out of the pulpit, honoring God. I was raised in a home that fostered a love for God. My dad didn't have my mom send the kids to church while he got ready to watch the football game. If Joshua was an American, he would have said, "as for me and my house, we're going to try to serve the Lord." Or he would have said, "I'm going to tell my wife to tell our kids to serve the Lord." Instead, Joshua, being the man of his home, told the whole congregation the following:

> Now fear the Lord and serve him with all
>   faithfulness. Throw away the gods your
>   ancestors worshiped beyond the
>   Euphrates River and in Egypt, and serve
>   the Lord. But if serving the Lord seems
>   undesirable to you, then choose for
>   yourselves this day whom you will

serve, whether the gods your ancestors
served beyond the Euphrates, or the
gods of the Amorites, in whose land you
are living. But as for me and my
household, we will serve the Lord.

— JOSHUA 24:14-15

At the beginning of 2021, I joined a gym because I didn't like the direction my body was trending and, I knew it wasn't going to reverse on its own. Did you know that all of our 14 employees at the time joined the gym right after I did? People do what you do. People do what the leader does. That's why a preacher can preach on soul winning until he's blue in the face, but if he doesn't go out and win souls, neither will the congregation. If you do what you tell people to do, you don't need to talk as much. For example, if you give, you don't need to teach much on giving. You replicate your behavior in others.

People do what you do, not always what you say. 85% of children will follow the spiritual example set by their father. Although you can't change America, you can take authority over the realm of your own home with your own children. As the man, God set you as the high priest over your home, and your children are spiritually connected with you. Spiritual fathers are wonderful and necessary. But a child doesn't need to go out and look for one when they have a Godly father in their home; one who didn't teach them how to buy weed and roll a joint, but rather a father who taught them the value of putting God first.

The Devil wants you to do the opposite of what God says in His Word. You meet people who are 55-years-old, and if you give them three minutes to talk, it won't be long before they get into how their dad was an alcoholic. Maybe he was, but you're 55, and it's time to turn the page. It's time to start saying that no matter what happened before, now I have the opportunity to change what the Devil meant for bad into a blessing by obeying God's Word. The Devil knows that a nation is only as strong as the families in that nation because the father is the high priest of the home. The enemy knows that if he can destroy the man's life, he has destroyed the people under him by default.

Solomon wrote good advice to his son in the book of Proverbs:

> My child, never forget the things I have
> taught you. Store my commands in your
> heart. If you do this, you will live many
> years, and your life will be satisfying.
>
> — PROVERBS 3:1-2

The Bible says there are things you can do to lengthen your life, and there are things you can do to shorten your life. Suppose I decided to quit the ministry today and go join a pagan motorcycle gang and start using meth. In that case, I'm probably not going to live as long as if I stayed doing what God called me to do. Life is not random. Life is based on the result of your choices and seeds that you sow.

> ...I see very clearly that God shows no
> favoritism. In every nation he accepts
> those who fear him and do what is right.
>
> — ACTS 10:34

God doesn't care what color your skin is. God doesn't care how many teeth you have or don't have. God doesn't care what your income is when you come to Him. God doesn't care if you have diseases. He cares to whom you give honor.

> I will honor those who honor me, and I will
> despise those who think lightly of me.
>
> — 1 SAMUEL 2:30B

So, what are the practical steps? These are not things my dad just taught me—these are things my dad role modeled for me.

NUMBER ONE

___

THE INCOMPREHENSIBLE VALUE OF THE WORD OF GOD

M y father showed me the incomprehensible value of the Word of God. My dad gave me a Bible when I was a little boy, and on the inside cover, he wrote, "This book will keep you from sin, and sin will keep you from this book." He also wrote 2 Timothy 2:20, *"If you keep yourself pure, you will be a vessel that's fit for an honorable use by the master."* And when that Bible was worn out, he would write the same thing in my next Bible. From my dad's example, I started reading the Bible at age six, basically as soon as I could read. I just grabbed it and started reading. My father showed me what I've learned about the Bible and how to be grounded in it. I'm a full-gospel, Pentecostal, charismatic, but charismatics are some of the flakiest people you'll ever meet.

"I need prayer."

"What do you need prayer for?"

"I don't feel saved."

Who cares. If you go by how you *feel* you're going to be in a mental institution. The Bible says the opposite—faith is not fear, but the opposite of faith is sight. We walk by faith and not by sight. Without faith, you gravitate to feelings.

"I feel depressed. I feel like I need a sabbatical."

You'll go to hell if you live by what you feel. The Devil will kick your tail from now until when you die. Instead, get the Devil in the arena of what God's Word says. In Luke chapter four, Jesus dealt with Satan himself. Satan came and said something to Him. Jesus answered, *"it is written."* Satan had no response.

The Devil has no answer for what is written in the Word. Base your life on the Word of God. There is no devil that can jerk with the Bible; it is an unbreakable foundation for life. That's why governments from Russia to China to California know that if you're going to destroy a generation, the Bible must be banned.

The Bible carries the power to make men champions. The Word of God will produce in you a hatred for sin. Not a "well, we shouldn't do that" sort of intolerance. Rather, as you read the Bible, God's Spirit gets in you, and you begin to hate what God hates and love what He loves. Somebody will invite you to a club, and they might as well be inviting you to help them move. "Nah, I'm okay."

It's hard to live Holy when you want to sin, but God's Word cleans that desire out of you and gives you a hatred for sin.

In the process of implanting God's Word in me, not only did my dad have me read the Bible, but he never talked me out of what it said. I would ask him, "Did Jesus really open the eyes of the blind?"

He would answer, "Yes, and He can still do that today."

My dad never did what many American Christians do, taking the scripture as figurative. He never said things like, "Jesus healed the blind, but today He just heals the spiritually blind." My dad taught me that if you take this book literally, it'll turn you into a world-changer.

NUMBER TWO

THE IMPORTANCE OF VALUING THE HOLY SPIRIT

My dad taught me the importance of valuing the Word and valuing the Holy Ghost, too. My family made a point to be in places where God's Spirit was present.

We were not like many American families where we had a "normal" church where we got out in 80 minutes guaranteed and another church for when someone needed a miracle.

We value the Holy Ghost. To this day, I don't care what the trends are in American, Canadian, or European Christianity. The Holy Ghost and I are partners, He's my number one partner, and He leads me. My dad taught me from a young age that the Holy Ghost will lead you by that still, small voice, and I leaned into it. When He convicts you or tells you, "Don't go there," never override it. And when He speaks to you, "This is the way," walk there and do what He says—immediately.

NUMBER THREE

THE VALUE OF PERSONAL RESPONSIBILITY

My dad taught me that God will do what He said He would do if I do my part. God did not write a book of promises; He wrote a covenant book. If you do what you're responsible for, God's committed to what He is responsible for, and God is too faithful to fail.

My father taught me the value of personal responsibility. I could never blame my teacher and get my dad to agree. I could never blame my coach and get my father to agree it was the coach's fault. "You produced the problem. You didn't get a D on your test because you have a bad teacher; you got a D on your test because you got a D on your test." While I hated it at the time, I'm thankful he taught me these truths because now I see people my age who can't hold a job because nobody can tell them anything. When they're late to work every day, they blame it on the traffic, then get fired because they've learned to blame everybody else.

When you get the father out of the home, the mother will usually defend the child. That's a mother's responsibility; she's like a mother bear. If you hit one of her babies, she does not care what the baby did to you first; the mother bear just kills you.

You can ask any public-school teacher, and they will tell you that now they can't even hold class because the kids can do whatever they want. And if they correct them, in comes the mother to ream out the teacher: "How dare you talk to my son like that!"

A father is supposed to teach their children that ultimately you bear responsibility for your life. For example, if I preach somewhere and have a bad meeting, I don't even blame the Devil. I am responsible for my life, and that makes me a good preacher. After a bad meeting, most preachers will say, "You know the Devil really has a stronghold in that area." No, you just blew it.

Fast and pray more. Get on your knees, and when you are in tandem with God, no one can stand against you for as long as you live.

Stop blaming demons; they're already under your feet. "You know, there's three witches that actually live in this town, and they've cursed this area." Oh, have they? They use the blood of chickens; we have the blood of Jesus. I'm supposed to be afraid of what they use?

There is a power in us far greater than all the power of hell put together. Charismatics would rule the world if they spent as much time focusing on what God said about the blessing that belongs to them as much as they focus on the curse.

Personal responsibility.

NUMBER FOUR

THE VALUE OF MY WORDS

The quickest way to get spanked in my household was to complain or to say something negative.

We were taught by example to use our words to speak faith. I was walking by an open hotel room on my way to the elevator in Allentown, Pennsylvania. I was going to preach on the power of our words. The Lord must have had me walk by that room just so I could hear how other people had it when not growing up in a preacher's home.

I heard a grandfather, who was in the hotel room with his son and his grandson, and he said, "You guys are going to see every year you get older, life gets harder." That's quite a prophecy to give to your son and your grandson.

Many people have never had anyone speak a blessing over them. In reality, at a young age, they had people in their own home telling them, "Wait until you're paying the rent on this place. You're having fun playing Nintendo, but wait until you get out and get a job."

Boys are growing up with fathers who tell them that women turn into dogs when you put a ring on their finger, that women are crazy. With their words, they set them up to expect defeat, and you get what you expect.

What happens when you begin to instruct your children in a Godly manner? "Do you see how good God has been to us? He's going to be even better to you because the blessing that's on me doesn't die with me. The Bible says it goes to my children and to my children's children."

NUMBER FIVE

THE POWER OF THANKFULNESS

Not only do you use your words to speak faith, but you also use your words to thank and magnify the Lord. When you complain, everything diminishes. When you begin to thank God, everything multiplies.

We didn't have a lot when I was growing up. My dad made $4,000 gross income his first year as an Evangelist, but I never heard him complain, and I never heard my mother complain. I saw them lift their hands and thank Jesus. I heard them say, "Thank you that somebody bought us McDonald's. Thank you that somebody filled our gas."

As we thanked God, I watched my dad increase. I saw a lady turn her home over to my dad; it had seven acres of property and was over 4,000 square feet. The lady said, "I was praying today, and the Lord spoke to me to give my home to you." And that was the home I spent the last two years in before I went to Bible school.

It doesn't matter where you start; you will finish high if you use your tongue to say, "Magnify the Lord and let us exalt His name forever."

Whatever you've lost in life, if you've lost anything, it's because of God that you haven't lost everything. So, as you begin to praise Him like Paul did in prison, your praise breaks you out of the dungeon. Your praise puts you on the high ground.

NUMBER SIX

FINISH WHAT YOU START

I wasn't allowed to quit any sport. Even if I didn't like it, I had to finish everything I started. If I didn't like the coach, I still had to finish the season.

If I joined a club, I had to stick with it until the end of the year, when it was over.

Now I can't quit anything. I even get convicted if I try to quit a video game early when I'm playing somebody online on Madden or FIFA.

Don't quit anything. Everything you start, you finish. Whether you get discouraged or feel sad, it doesn't matter. Everything you set out to do, you see it through until the end.

My dad instilled something in me that says you stay with everything until it is complete, even in small things.

NUMBER SEVEN

THE VALUE OF HEAVEN'S REWARD

S omething I don't hear preached much anymore is that this life is but a vapor. We are here today and gone tomorrow, and one day we will stand before the Lord to give an account for what we've done in this body. That has not only kept me from sin but has also kept me straight on what I preach.

If you're driven by what people like, you'll end up with a nothing ministry. But if you understand that one day, you'll give an account to God for what you did with His Word and what He called you to do, you'll be motivated in ministry.

The Bible says in 1 Corinthians 3 that every man will present his work. Everyone will present his work to the Lord and either receive a reward or barely make heaven. And that's the people that Jesus will have to wipe the tears from their eyes. They'll realize they spent seven decades of their life and did nothing that God set before them to do.

But that will never be you from today forward; everything you do will impact eternity in some way.

NUMBER EIGHT

THE REALITY OF HELL

The last thing my father instilled in me is that there's not only heaven as a reward, but there is also hell as punishment.

You shouldn't want to get saved just so you won't go to hell, although we won't go to hell if we are saved. But if avoiding hell were the only reason to get saved, it would be worth getting your rear end saved.

You hear preachers say, "How many of you know the worst thing about hell will be being separated from God forever?" No, it won't be. What would you care if you were separated from God for eternity when you never knew Him to begin with?

In Luke 16:23-25, the rich man didn't say, "Oh, I long for the presence of God." He said, *"Father Abraham, have some pity! Send Lazarus over here to dip the tip of his finger in water and cool my tongue. I am in anguish in these flames."* Then, when he realized he couldn't get out, he wanted to send somebody to his father's home to warn his brothers. Isn't it amazing that a guy who never had time for God his entire life then wanted to be an evangelist? *"Tell my brothers to get their act together so they don't come here."*

"Your brothers can open the Bible and read Moses and the prophets anytime they want."

People will be held accountable for what they do with God's Word.

I was listening to an evangelist from Ghana who asked the question to ministers, "When was the last time you ever preached a message on salvation? Not just mentioned salvation in your message, but preached an entire message on sin separating man from God and men being reconciled by Jesus and His blood on the cross so they can go to heaven. And that if they don't receive Jesus, they will spend an eternity in hell."

There really is a heaven. There really is a hell. Every person will spend their eternity in one of those two places.

Where you spend eternity is not dictated by God. God has voted for you; sin and Satan have voted against you. You cast the deciding ballot. You can do nothing and go to hell. Or you can say, "I'm not going to hell. I make up my mind today."

The number one goal of a Christian is not to win souls but to make heaven yourself. Paul, in 1 Corinthians 9 said, "*I keep a close watch on myself, what I teach and how I live.*"

I've made up my mind from this day forward, in the name of Jesus, no matter what the Devil has aligned against me, I will finish well.

You can do the same.

AFTERWORD

It would be impossible for me to not end up serving the Lord and loving Him with all my heart because I was raised in a home where my mom and dad didn't just preach from a pulpit – they walked out their faith.

They didn't speak one way while preaching, then turn and live the opposite way. 85% of people follow the spiritual example of their father, your children do what you do more than they do what you say. The father is the leader of the home, this design was set up by God.

People do what the leader does, you replicate your behavior in others. If you're strung out on drugs, your children will be too. But if you honor the Lord and put value on spending time with Him and in His house, your children will too. That's exactly what my parents did in raising my sister and I.

Take any violent offender from a jail, and give them the father I had growing up, and they wouldn't end up in that prison. I didn't have a dad teaching me how to roll a joint or how to make meth, I had a father teaching me the value of putting God first, the value of learning the Word of God.

Your life is based off the choices that you make, life is not a random hand of cards dealt to you. God doesn't discriminate based on your skin color, your age, your backstory, or even how many teeth you have left in your head, He cares about who you honor.

God outlined what you can do to lengthen your life and what is expected of you as a man of God. These are the lessons my father role modeled for me and everything a man should be; the incomprehensible value of the Word of God, the importance of valuing the Holy Spirit, the value of personal responsibility, the value of my words, the power of thankfulness, the importance of finishing what you start, the value of heaven's reward, and the reality of hell.

"*My generation shall be saved!*"

— JONATHAN
SHUTTLESWORTH

ABOUT THE AUTHOR

Evangelist and Pastor, Jonathan Shuttlesworth, is the founder of Revival Today and Pastor of Revival Today Church, ministries dedicated to reaching lost and hurting people with The Gospel of Jesus Christ.

In fulfilling his calling, Jonathan Shuttlesworth has conducted meetings and open-air crusades throughout North America, India, the Caribbean, and Central and South Africa.

Revival Today Church was launched in 2022 as a soul-winning, Holy Spirit honoring church that is unapologetic about believing the Bible to bless families and nations.

Each day thousands of lives are impacted globally through Revival Today Broadcasting and Revival Today Church, located in Pittsburgh, Pennsylvania.

While methods may change, Revival Today's heartbeat remains for the lost, providing biblical teaching on faith, healing, prosperity, freedom from sin, and living a victorious life.

If you need help or would like to partner with Revival Today to see this generation and nation transformed through The Gospel, follow these links…

CONTACT REVIVAL TODAY

www.RevivalToday.com
www.RevivalTodayChurch.com

facebook.com/revivaltoday
twitter.com/jdshuttlesworth
instagram.com/jdshuttlesworth
youtube.com/RevivalToday07

CPSIA information can be obtained
at www.ICGtesting.com
Printed in the USA
BVHW041435240922
647685BV00003B/19

9 781644 572832